If Only

Deborah Weed

For Benjamin, my beloved dad

ISBN -979-8-218-14298-8

The text of this book is set in 16 point Palatino Bold.
The illustrations were created by AI and Deborah Weed's Digital Art.
Book Design by Deborah Weed

Faith took a deep breath. Today, stardust seeds were becoming snowflakes. Faith, the keeper of all belief, knew that these seemingly minute wisps were about to leap into the unknown. Little did they know that it would take all of their courage.

One of the prismatic molecules of Divinity caught Faith's attention. She flitted and flurried with a rhythm that was all her own.

"Who am I?" asked Snowflake.

Faith lifted her head and replied, "You are the reflection of me, a whisper in my heart. My very breath. Are you ready to take your leap?"

"My leap? Where am I going?" Snowflake asked.

"On a journey to becoming!" answered Faith. "Always remember, only by falling will you be lifted."

Snowflake hesitated and leaned backwards.

"IF ONLY I could stay with you, instead of jumping into uncertainty," Snowflake cried out.

"IF ONLY you knew," Faith chimed in.

At first Snowflake felt the pure exhilaration of a free fall. As she tumbled farther, the caressing warmth of the sun entered her very core. The sacred hexagon shape began to whirl faster and faster. She felt abuzz as her pulse quickened.

Snowflake drifted to and fro, as if dancing to a melodic waltz. Cold damp air met with heat, forcing crystalline branches to sprout. She watched the spectacle of her budding kaleidoscopic crystals as they blossomed. In spite of herself, she misted over with joy.

Snowflake E X P A N D E D .

As Snowflake plummeted farther into the Earth's atmosphere, a breeze tickled her.

She heard a shrill honking sound in the distance. It startled Snowflake. Thousands of snow geese were making their way toward her. Snowflake tried to lift herself upwards. She wanted to avoid colliding with the blizzard of white birds. It was too late.

"Whouk! Whouk! Look out!" shouted a baby chick flying alongside his mother.

Snowflake watched as the baby snow goose flapped his wings. The snowstorm of geese all flew in unison.

With a frantic intensity, Snowflake flapped her pristine branches. It caused her to go in circles.

"I can't seem to control where I'm going," cried Snowflake. Dizziness made her woozy

The baby goose effortlessly glided by. "You can't fly? he asked.

"I don't have wings. I only have these icy branches," said Snowflake.

"Why can't Snowflake come with us?" the baby snow goose asked his mom.

"Snowflake doesn't have wings like us. She can't go where she wants to. Only where the winds of chance take her," chirped the baby goose's mother.

"IF ONLY I could fly," Snowflake shouted into the choppy wind. She watched the geese disappear as they flew south.

Although invisible, Faith had never left Snowflake's side.

"AND THEN you'd never discover," explained Faith, "that not everyone has the ability to fly, but that doesn't mean you can't soar. Instead of focusing on what you cannot do, embrace what you can do and let your talents shine. Remember, the beauty of life is in its diversity and everyone has their own unique way of reaching new heights."

As Snowflake twirled downwards, her branches collected more crystals. The spectacle of it, at least momentarily, made her heart jump for joy.

A cloud of mist obscured her view. Snowflake felt it before she saw it. There was a slight bounce and then a bit of a prickle. Millions of other snowflakes joined her at the tiptop of a giant sequoia tree. She was over 200 feet above the ground, cushioned by snow-covered forest green needles. Snowflake was afraid to move.

There was stillness. From her lofty position, Snowflake could see a strong, rooted trunk. It was 22 feet in diameter with etched bark and embellished with burls. A new-found strength spread throughout her own branches.

"Welcome little one," said Sequoia.

"I feel so safe up here. You are so strong," exclaimed Snowflake.

"That's what happens when you live for over 3,000 years. I've experienced a lot in my lifetime," said Sequoia. He photosynthesized all of his memories.

"Will I live a long time?" Snowflake asked.

"Do you have roots?" Sequoia inquired, as his limbs swayed in the breeze.

"What are they? What are roots?" asked Snowflake.

"Roots help you keep grounded. They allow you to weather both the good times and bad ones," answered Sequoia.

Snowflake giggled. "Well, I'm certainly not grounded if I'm way up here in your bough."

"Too bad," said Sequoia, as he began to shake her off.

Snowflake tried to steady herself. Her stardust branches did not bend like those of the tree. She floated toward the ground.

"IF ONLY I had roots so that I could stay in one place for my entire lifetime," pined Snowflake.

"AND THEN you would never realize," Faith said, as she rustled through the trees, "that change is not always easy, but it is necessary for growth. Although roots may seem to be the answer, they are not necessary for you to be grounded. It's more important to be centered in your own being. Embrace the unknown, dear one, and have faith that new opportunities and adventures await you. Trust in yourself and your abilities to navigate through any challenges that come your way. Remember, wherever you go, you take a part of yourself with you, and leave a part of yourself behind. Embrace the journey and have the courage to create a new path, for it is through change that we truly discover who we are."

As Snowflake bid Sequoia adieu, she heard a drumming sound. A woodpecker warned, "Pee-dee-dink, pee-dink. Be careful, all water-one. I saw people down there."

"People? What's a people?" asked Snowflake.

Snowflake was crestfallen. She had no wings to carry her or roots to nourish her diamond dust. Snowflake leaned into the wind. Her bravado was dissolving. Other flurrying snowflakes wanted to get nearer and comfort her, but her finely sculptured points kept them from getting too close.

As Snowflake floated nearer to the ground, she heard full-bodied laughter for the first time. The sound of utter happiness bounced off the trees and stirred up all living things.

A brother and sister watched in awe. Their beaming wide-eyed faces looked upwards, waiting for the heavens to sprinkle them with wonder. It seemed as if they were waiting for HER.

Snowflake pushed back her branches so that she was on full display. The little girl, with a head of strawberry curls that bounced in time with her enthusiasm, put out a finger to break Snowflake's fall. Like a beauty queen in a parade, Snowflake sparkled and waved her arms.

"Look, this is the most beautiful snowflake EVER! No two snowflakes in the whole-entire-world are the same. You're a miracle in action," exclaimed the little girl as Snowflake landed. She put her rosy cheeks so close that Snowflake could feel her warmth.

Is this what love feels like? wondered Snowflake.

Suddenly, the little girl's brother said, "Hurry up and make a snowball before the snow melts!"

What's melt, thought Snowflake. Her entire being trembled. Snowflake began to cry. She didn't want anything to change. Her hexagon form began to vanish. Snowflake's earthly beauty was softening and her inner glow dimmed.

The little girl with the strawberry curls lovingly patted her on the back while picking up more snow to make a firm white snowball.

"IF ONLY I could be loved like this for the rest of my life," sighed Snowflake.

"AND THEN you'd never learn that although heartache can be difficult to bear, the love that surrounds you is eternal and will always be with you," murmured Faith.

Snowflake softened along with the other snowflakes. She curled up into the snowball. Together, they were hurled into the air, as if being tossed away. She felt herself hit the little boy at full force and then she splashed onto the glistening ground.

As Snowflake melted, the heat turned her to slush. Some snowflakes seeped into the soggy ground to nourish the plants. Others, along with Snowflake, merged together and trickled down a hill toward a prancing, humming brook. She lost sight of the little girl she had just begun to love!

The surging snowflakes pushed Snowflake closer to the stream. A whooshing sound crashed around her as she became part of the current. Now watery, she was swept away. She had a choice, either fight against the undertow, or go with the flow.

SNOWFLAKE
LET GO!

A milky fog made it impossible to see clearly. Snowflake could feel the spray of gushing water force her upwards into the air. She evaporated.

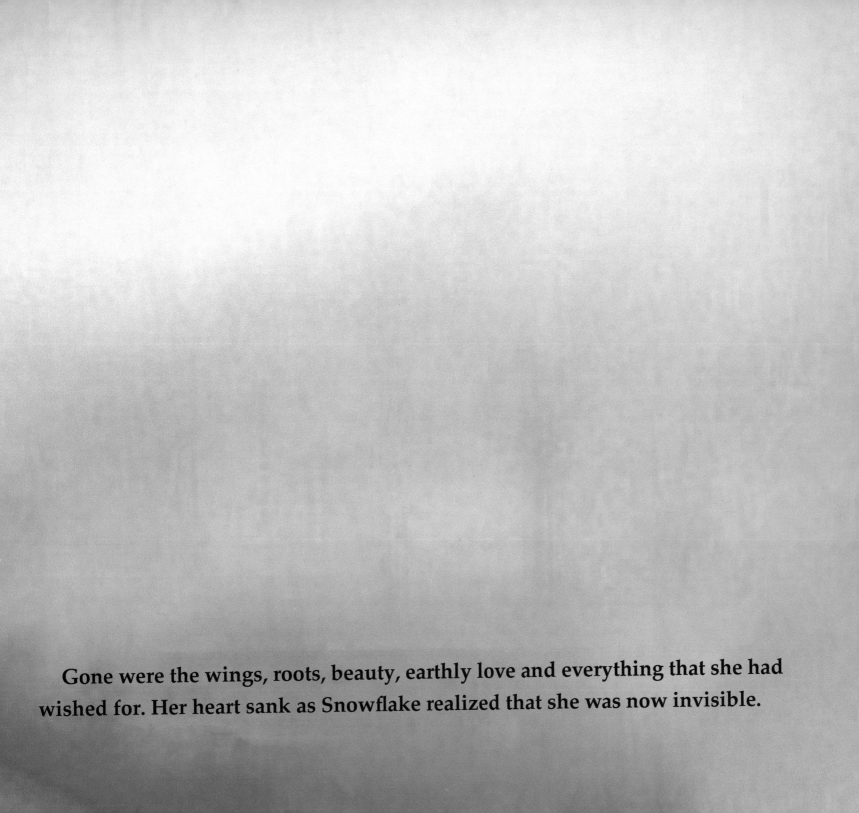

Gone were the wings, roots, beauty, earthly love and everything that she had wished for. Her heart sank as Snowflake realized that she was now invisible.

"IF ONLY I weren't transparent," lamented Snowflake. The entire world seemed to stop spinning. . .

At that moment, Faith's shock of hair morphed into a brilliant rainbow. Being translucent allowed ALL THAT IS to shine through Snowflake.

"AND THEN you would never see that you are not melting away into nothingness, but rather, you are becoming part of something greater. . . Your beauty and unique form may evolve but your essence will always be with the earth, the sky, and the sea. You will continue to be a part of the cycle of life, providing nourishment and life to the world. Remember that every snowflake is unique and special, just like you. Embrace the change and know that your existence has a purpose and value," shared Faith.

Snowflake felt glorious multi-colored sunlight refract through her. First rose red, and then sunflower orange, followed by lemon yellow, leaf green, sapphire blue, indigo and then sunset violet. She rode Faith's rainbow, billowing hair along with all the other vaporized snowflakes.

"IF ONLY I had known that I was never alone!" shouted Snowflake as her essence sparkled with glee.

"My dear Snowflake, do not let regrets cloud your mind. Always remember,
IF ONLY...YOU KNEW HOW MUCH YOU ARE LOVED. . .
all would be well. Allow the love that surrounds you to guide and heal you,"
beamed Faith.

AND THEN, they shot up toward the North Star. IF ONLY Snowflake knew what was next!

CPSIA information can be obtained
at www.ICGtesting.com
Printed in the USA
LVHW071757130423
744294LV00009B/430